D0090353

THE RALPH WIGGUM BOOK

THE SIMPSONS™ LIBRARY OF WISDOM
THE RALPH WIGGUM BOOK

Copyright © 2005 by
Bongo Entertainment, Inc. and Matt Groening Productions, Inc. All rights reserved.

Printed in the USA.
No part of this book may be used or reproduced in any manner whatsoever without written permission except in the case of brief quotations embodied in critical articles and reviews. For information address
HarperCollins Publishers,
10 East 53rd Street, New York, NY 10022.

HarperCollins books may be purchased for educational, business, or sales promotional use. For information please write:
Special Markets Department,
HarperCollins Publishers,
10 East 53rd Street, New York, NY 10022.

FIRST EDITION

ISBN-10: 0-06-074820-6
ISBN-13: 978-0-06-074820-3

05 06 07 08 09 10 WOR 10 9 8 7 6 5 4 3 2 1

Publisher: Matt Groening
Creative Director: Bill Morrison
Managing Editor: Terry Delegeane
Director of Operations: Robert Zaugh
Art Director: Nathan Kane
Special Projects Art Director: Serban Cristescu
Production Manager: Christopher Ungar
Production/Design: Karen Bates, Art Villanueva
Staff Artists: Chia-Hsien Jason Ho, Mike Rote
Production Assistant: Nathan Hamill
Administration: Sherri Smith
Legal Guardian: Susan A. Grode

THE SIMPSONS™ LIBRARY OF WISDOM

Conceived and Edited by Bill Morrison
Book Design and Production by Serban Cristescu
Contributing Editor: Terry Delegeane
Research and Production Assistance: Nathan Hamill

Contributing Artists:
Edwin Aguilar, Karen Bates, John Costanza, Melanie Cristescu, Serban Cristescu, Mike DeCarlo, John Delaney, Becca Emanuel, Luis Escobar, Nathan Hamill, Nathan Kane, Mike Kazaleh, Jorge Laurenco, James Lloyd, Istvan Majoros, Jeanette Moreno, Bill Morrison, Kevin M. Newman, Phil Ortiz, Andrew Pepoy, Mike Rote, Kevin Segna, Robert Stanley, Ty Templeton, Eric Tran, Chris Ungar, Art Villanueva

Contributing Writers:
James W. Bates, Tony DiGerolamo, Scott M. Gimple, Nathan Hamill, Jesse L. McCann, Bill Morrison, Tom Peyer, Ty Templeton, Mary Trainor, Patric M. Verrone

Special Thanks to:
Pete Benson, N. Vyolet Diaz, Deanna MacLellan, Helio Salvatierra, Mili Smythe, and Ursula Wendel

THE RALPH WIGGUM BOOK

Harper

An Imprint of Harper Collins*Publishers*

1. KITTY LITTER.
2. TRAINING PANTS.
3. THE COLOR BURPLE.
4. MY HOME MOMMY.
5. MY SCHOOL MOMMY, MS. HOOVER.
6. GETTING SMARTERER AND BEING THE BESTEST.
7. PLAYING VIKING MUSIC ON MY NOSE FLUTE.
8. TREE SAP.
9. PASTE.
10. THE FUNNY THINGS THE LEPRECHAUN TELLS ME TO DO.
11. DRY PAJAMAS.
12. WHALE EGGS.
13. PUTTING STUFF IN MY NOSE.
14. FINDING STUFF IN MY NOSE.
15. TAKING STUFF OUT OF MY NOSE.
16. LISA SIMPSON.
17. HUGGY PEOPLE ON CABLE TV.
18. CATERPILLARS, PRINCETIPAL SKINNER, AND MY DADDY.
19. BOVINE U.
20. SMELL-O-VISION.
21. LEARNING NEW WORDS, LIKE "NEW" AND "WORD."
22. SPONGES THAT TASTE LIKE MOMMY'S COOKING.
23. THE TALKING MATCHSTICKS.
24. COUNTING UP TO ONE.
25. MY HAIRDO. IT'S SPECIAL!
26. BOOKS FOR DUMMIES.
27. TOENAILS AND JELL-O.
28. LEFTOVER CAT FOOD.
29. WORMS.
30. GETTING DE-WORMED.
31. RE-WORMING.
32. BUS FUMES.
33. YUMMY THUMBTACKS.
34. FINDING LUMPY THINGS IN MY MASHED POTATOES.
35. THE SMELL OF SPIT UP MILK ON A SUMMER'S DAY.
36. DID I MENTION LISA SIMPSON ALREADY?
37. CORN NUT BREATH.
38. SPIROCHETES.
39. AQUARIUM GRAVEL.
40. WEARING A BATHROBE WHEN I'M NOT EVEN SICK.

A TYPICAL DAY IN THE LIFE

7:00 a.m. – Wakes up. Washes face, brushes teeth. Removes "Police Cop"® brand PJs, folds nicely, puts on foot of bed. Leaves house, ready for new day.

7:15 a.m. - Spotted by Ned Flanders walking down boulevard completely naked, declaring, "I'm the Woodstock baby!" Horrified, Flanders returns "Rude-nude-diddily-dude" home to parents.

7:20 a.m. - Gets dressed.

7:30 a.m. - Mommy redresses him. Reminds him which limb is supposed to go through which hole.

7:40 a.m. - Breakfast time. Finds free Krusty Steel Marble® in cereal box. Puts up left nostril for safekeeping.

7:45 a.m. - Daddy notices that free steel marble is nowhere to be found. Vows to dutifully inspect "evidence bowl" every night until it turns up.

7:50 a.m. - Misses school bus by standing on wrong side of street. Must walk to school. Walks wrong way.

8:00 a.m.- Stops at bus bench to sit on lap of fat, long-haired, bearded homeless person. Recites list of toys he wants for Christmas.

8:05 a.m. - Chief Wiggum spots Ralph holding hair of fat man who is barfing into trash can. Decides to drive his son to school.

8:10 a.m. - Daddy lets him blast siren. Frightened octogenarian in front of them rams his car into mayor's limo.

8:20 a.m. - Ralph arrives late for school again. Principal Skinner makes mention of it in "Hopelessly Special Students" notebook.

OF RALPH WIGGUM

8:30 a.m. - "Show and Tell" time. Shows phlegm-encrusted hanky he received as Christmas present that morning. Tells everyone Santa smells like pee-pee.

8:45 a.m. - Tells Miss Hoover she does not look well. Wonders aloud if she has "Glug-glug Flu" that Daddy says she catches at nightclubs two/three times a week. Miss Hoover tells Ralph to rest his head inside desk.

9:00 a.m. - History lesson. Ralph forgot to do his history homework again. As punishment, Miss Hoover makes him sit on stool, facing corner to stare at walls.

9:10 a.m. - Ralph daydreams he is Lord Raglan, British hero of Waterloo, commanding his Crimean War armies, driving Russians out of Wallachia/Moldavia by end of summer 1854...

9:30 a.m. - Miss Hoover taps Ralph's shoulder with pointer, tells him to return to desk; says he is terrible at history, always will be. Teacher's sudden interruption/caustic criticism drive Crimean War thoughts deep into lizard-brain area of Ralph's memory, never to be dredged up again.

10:00 a.m. - "Arts and Crafts" time. Ralph glues his chin to his elbow. Groundskeeper Willie must separate body parts with crowbar.

10:15 a.m. - Recess. Loses battle with tetherball. Groundskeeper Willie must untie him from pole.

11:00 a.m. - Class field trip: lunch at Springfield Airport. Second grade students grab sack lunches then board the bus. Ralph forgot sack lunch, instead grabs bag belonging to Miss Hoover containing tampons/lighter fluid/bottle of Percocet.

11:15 a.m. - Arrive at airport. Last in line, Ralph stopped by security guards at beeping metal detector. Unaware, Miss Hoover's class continues into airport.

11:20 a.m. - Security wand indicates something metal hidden in Ralph's head. Officer moves Ralph to area for "cavity search." Screaming fear of dentist ensues. Escapes on conveyor belt through tiny door.

11:25 a.m. - Security calls for emergency lock-down of airport. As precaution, school bus in parking lot searched. Security personnel find Miss Hoover's bag that Ralph left behind. Otto arrested for possession of drugs/flammable liquid/cotton explosive fuses.

11:30 a.m. - Security police begin extensive search of tarmac. Springfield Air Flight 1955 nonstop to Paris takes off with Ralph sitting in galley behind carts of food.

11:40 a.m. - Ralph exits galley to main cabin. Finds empty seat next to man with extreme fear of flying. Asks man what time movie starts.

11: 45 a.m. - Man tells Ralph he paid for empty seat next to him so he can be alone. Ralph picks his nose and wipes snot on man's pillow. Says man smells like "old pepperoni pizza."

12:00 p.m. - Ralph quickly drives man insane. When Ralph won't stop fussing with lunch condiments, man grabs cabin attendant, puts plastic spoon to her throat, demands to be taken to Cuba.

12:05 p.m. - Spilled pepper makes Ralph sneeze explosively. Free Krusty Steel Marble® shoots out his nose, hits hijacker in forehead. Hijacker knocked unconscious. Attendant faints.

12:15 p.m. - Cockpit crew become aware something is amiss in main cabin when they hear "Would you like fries with that?" and "Please drive forward, Mr. Customer" repeatedly over plane P.A. system.

12:45 p.m. - Springfield Air Flight 1955 makes emergency landing back at Springfield Airport. Ralph disembarks, blends in with classmates just leaving.

12:50 p.m. - Miss Hoover, furious Otto is missing, has to drive bus herself. Ralph breaks out in spontaneous rendition of "B-I-N-G-O"—spelling "Bingo" incorrectly.

1:05 p.m. - Class returns to Springfield Elementary. Principal Skinner makes "Hopelessly Special Students" note that Ralph apparently was forced to ride in bus luggage compartment on way back.

1:20 p.m. - Assembly: Talent Show. Springfield Cable Access videotapes as Ralph plays "Greensleeves" with flute stuck up nose. Lisa Simpson surprises everyone by adding improvisational dance to Ralph's performance.

1:55 p.m. - School out. Kids must walk home as Otto still has not returned. Ralph walks wrong way.

2:10 p.m. - Bart Simpson tricks Ralph into going through revolving door of Costington's Department Store. Gets stuck going around for twenty minutes. Says stomach feels "squirmy."

2:30 p.m. - Freed from revolving doors by store manager, continues walk home. Progress slow as he circles each block several times.

2:45 p.m. - Sarah Wiggum calls Chief, concerned that Ralph is not home from school. Chief puts out All Point Bulletin.

2:55 p.m. - Officers Lou/Eddie spot Ralph circling parking meter, pick him up, allow him to blast siren. Octogenarian in front of them has anxiety attack, sideswiping several cars as he makes left turn into Department of Motor Vehicles parking lot.

3:10 p.m. - Dropped off at Police Station. To pass time, Daddy lets him practice tasering criminals in cell. Incarcerated hijacker and Otto beg for mercy.

4:00 p.m. - Arrives home with Daddy. Plays in backyard until supper, eats pill bugs from under rock, has Wiggle Puppy adventure called "Rusty Nail in Board." Leprechaun instructs him to burn Daddy's socks/underwear.

5:00 p.m. - Otherwise lighthearted dinner somewhat dampened by smell of smoking socks/underwear in microwave.

5:15 p.m. - Bath time. Gets into frothy, bubbly tub. Forgets to remove clothing.

6:00 p.m. - Watches TV with family. Cable access program reveals Lisa Simpson not dancing to Ralph's nose-flute solo, instead she is trying to dodge flying boogers. "America's Most Armed and Dangerous" marathon follows.

8:00 p.m. - Bedtime. Washes face, brushes teeth. Removes "Police Cop"® brand PJs, folds nicely, puts on foot of bed, hops in. "Lights out, Cadet!"

11:00 p.m. - Chief Wiggum grabs bike, heads out door after Kent Brockman TV report about naked boy driving police cruiser through town. Wiggum kisses wife goodbye. Says, "Oh, that boy of ours!"

The Many Emotions of

DELIGHT   CONFUSION   SHOCK

CONFIDENCE   SURPRISE   ANXIETY

RALPH WIGGUM

WONDER   EUPHORIA   ANGER

DREAD   AWE   COMFORT

Ralph's Poetry Corner

The Little Ringworm

I have a little ringworm with tiny ruby rings.
He plays among my head and hair and in my ear he sings.
He dances on my scalp and skin so happy all the day,
And then he spreads his scabby wings and softly flakes away.

Monday

I ate a little mud pie,
And then I ate some ants.
I drank out of the fish tank,
And then I wet my pants.

I Dress Myself

I dress myself
In togs so tight,
Mommy thinks I'm
A water sprite!

I shoe myself
In shoes so shined,
Daddy thinks
He's going blind!

I undress myself
On our front lawn,
Neighbors think I'm
A leprechaun!

Snowflakes

This snowflake tastes like fish sticks.
This one tastes like stew.
This snowflake tastes like cake mix.
This one tastes like -- Eeeewwww!

The Other Little Ringworm

The roses are angry.
The violets are, too.
My head is scratchy.
I need a shampoo.

Friday

I passed the schoolyard bullies,
Who grabbed me by my shirt,
Then they stole my money,
And pushed me in the dirt.

My Little Nose

Pickety pick!
My little nose!
It gets picked
Like a red, red rose.
Sometimes once,
And sometimes twice,
It gets picked
'Cause it's so nice!

Saturday

I ate a smelly toadstool,
Like a happy little elf.
I danced around the meadow,
And then I soiled myself.

A Special Boy

If all the boys were a boy like me,
What a special boy we would be!
We'd eat pie and smell all funky.
We would buy us all a monkey!

If all the boys were a boy like me,
Who would chase us up the tree?
Who would tease and pull our hair?
Who would laugh at our underwear?

How could our mommies tell us apart?
Would my daddy know me from Bart?
If all the boys were a boy like me...
Stop! This poem is scaring me!

Sunday

I saw a little bluebird
A-sitting on its perch.
It poopied on my haircut
While on my way to church.

I Like Paste!

I like the taste
Of paste,
And the way
It tastes
Like paste.

Red, Pink, Blue, and Green

I had some red pajamas,
Some pajamas that were red.
I put them on upside-down,
And then I went to bed.

I had some pink wormies,
Some wormies that were pink.
I put them in my cocoa,
And then I had a drink.

I had some blue Band-Aids
Some Band-Aids that were blue.
I peeled them off my owie,
And then I ate them, too.

I had a green something,
Something that was green.
I put it in my tummy,
And now I don't feel so good,
And I don't want to write any more poems.

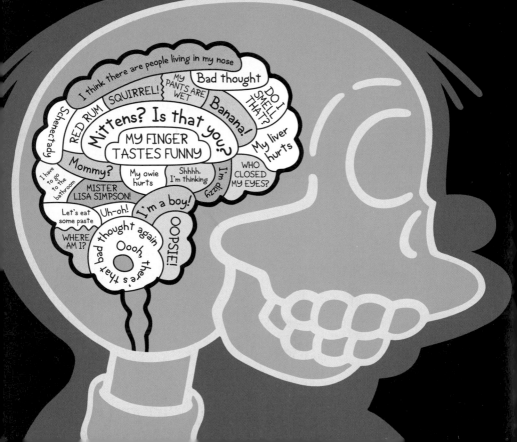

WHAT'S ON RALPH'S MIND?

THE WISDOM OF RALPH
If rice is wriggling, it's not rice.
A puppy can grow up to be president of America, but a kitten cannot.
If you put something far enough back in your nose, it will come out your mouth.
When I'm sick, my tummy makes floor soup.

MOMMY MAKES MY LUNCH ON **NORMAL** SCHOOL DAYS, BUT WHEN YOU'RE A GROWN UP, SATURDAYS ARE FOR **SNOOZING**. THAT'S THE DAY **I** MAKE **MY OWN** LUNCH TO SHARE WITH MY **HOBO TEACHERS** AT TRAIN YARD SCHOOL. NOW YOU CAN TOO, WITH THESE EASY TO FOLLOW...

LUNCH BOX RESTIPEES!

Deviled Eggs

Ingredients:
- eggs
- mayonnaise
- paprika
- Satan

PREPARATION:
Get six hard-boiled eggs.
Mix them up with some mayonnaise.
Sprinkle on some paprika.
Offer them to Satan.

Cat Food Salad

INGREDIENTS:
- cat food
- relish
- mayonnaise

PREPARATION:
Mix together in a bowl.
Chill and Serve.

Filly Steak Sandwich

INGREDIENTS:
- racehorse
- bell peppers
- swiss cheese
- onion
- roll

PREPARATION:
Have Daddy bring one home from the track.

Hot Diggety Dog

INGREDIENTS:
- hot dog
- mud

PREPARATION:
Get a HOT DOG.
Roll it in the mud.

Aquarium Gravel in a Cloud

INGREDIENTS:
- Aquarium gravel
- vanilla pudding
- whipped cream

PREPARATION:
Get some Aquarium gravel.
Put it in some pudding.
Top with whipped cream.

Corn Dogs

INGREDIENTS:
- corn on the cob
- dog food

PREPARATION:
Get a corn on the cob.
Spread some of the dog's
  food on it.
Don't let the dog
catch you doing this.

Crunchy Munchies

INGREDIENTS:
- dirt
- twigs
- paste

PREPARATION:
Get a twig.
Spread paste over it.
Stick it in the dirt.

Daddy's Phony Baloney Sandwich

INGREDIENTS:
- baloney
- malarkey
- hogwash
- a load of hooey
- Bread

PREPARATION:
Eat it and be quiet, Kid!

S'morez No Mores

INGREDIENTS:
- marshmallows
- Graham crackers
- brown Crayons

PREPARATION:
Put marshmallows and brown crayons
together in pan on stovetop.
Simmer for 5 minutes.
Let cool.
Pour onto cracker.

Chicken à la Viking

INGREDIENTS:
- Chicken pot pie
- Swedish meat
- Danish pastry

PREPARATION:
Mix ingredients together in your lunch box.
Leave it in your backpack over the weekend.
Share with friends on Monday.

Smashed Potatoes

INGREDIENTS:
- potatoes
- regrets

PREPARATION:

Go to fridge.
Get a bowl of Leftover mashed Potatoes.
Sit down on curb outside to eat it.

Have bullies shove your face in it.

Ants on a Log

INGREDIENTS:
- ants
- stick
- paste

PREPARATION:
Get a stick about 5 inches Long.
Spread Paste over the stick.
Sprinkle ants onto Paste.

Mommy's tired of making Lunches

INGREDIENT?:
- $5.00

PREPARATION:

Get yourself something at the cafeteria.

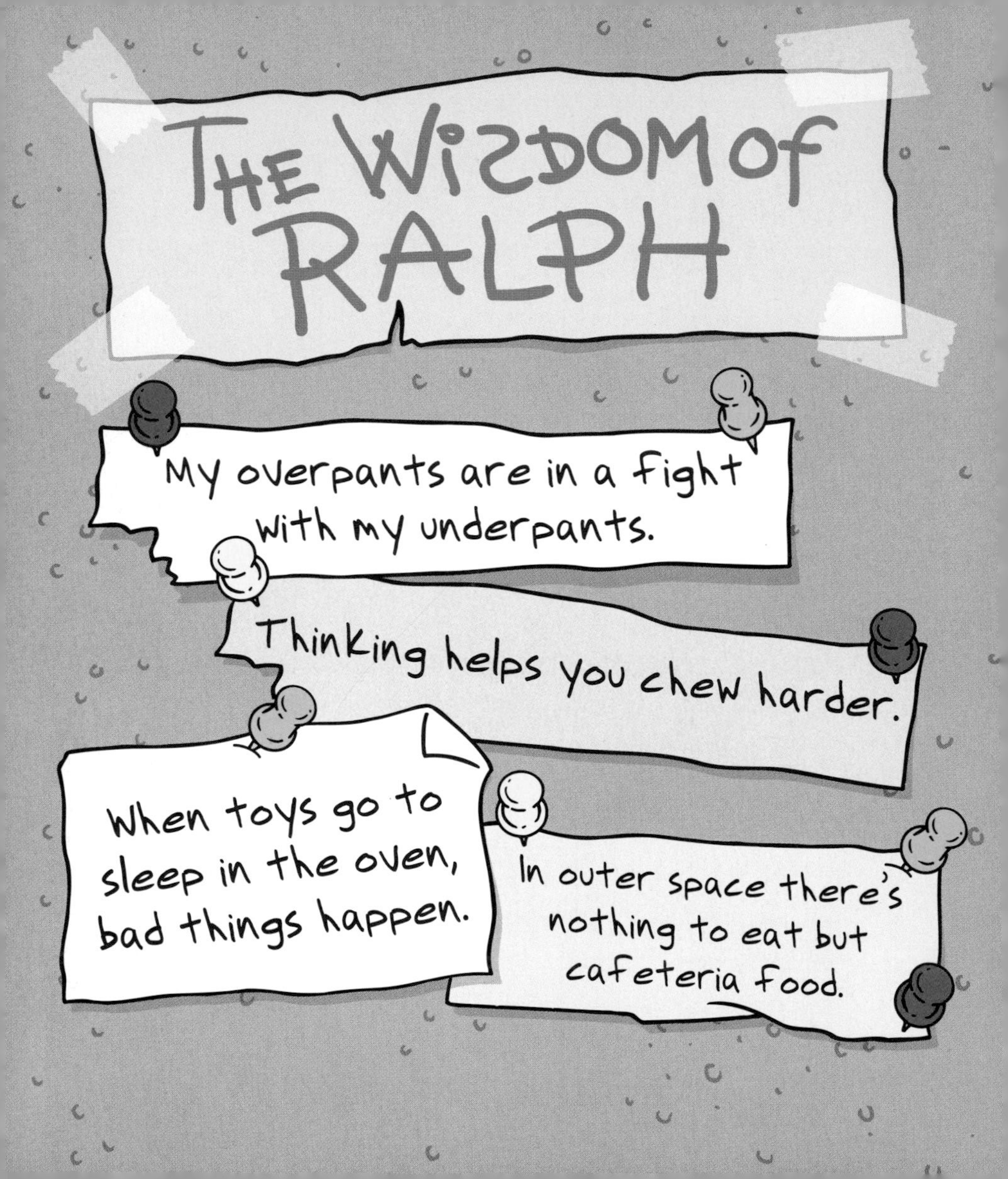
THE WISDOM OF RALPH
My overpants are in a fight with my underpants.
Thinking helps you chew harder.
When toys go to sleep in the oven, bad things happen.
In outer space there's nothing to eat but cafeteria food.

SNIFFING UP
SOME SAFETY

a Wiggle Puppy Adventure

Wiggle Puppy was ready for another adventure! He trotted out of his doghouse, jumped into the air, and took off for the sky, "Arf! Arf! Vrooom!"

Wiggle Puppy used Wiggle-Power to fly. All he had to do was shake his behind, and his tail and ears would start twirling like helicopter blades.

"Vrooom! Vrooom! Arf!" Wiggle Puppy announced, as he flew high over Springfield. This was his way of saying, "I am on another adventure, ready to serve anyone who needs me!"

Soon Wiggle Puppy's keen eyes spotted a man riding a bicycle below him. The man had no helmet and was in imminent danger. Wiggle Puppy knew it was his duty to save him!

"Vroom! Arf! Vroom!" Wiggle Puppy shouted, which was his way of saying, "Don't worry, sir! I am coming to assist you!"

The man was very confused when Wiggle Puppy descended from the sky and flew in tight circles around his head.

"Wha--?!" the man said. "Oh, it's you, there...that Wiggly Dog."

Wiggle Puppy barked, licked the man's face, and flew in circles again. At first the man smiled nervously, but very soon he started to get cross with Wiggle Puppy.

"What are ya doin'?" The man was kind of wobbly on his bicycle. "Stop buzzin' around me! I'm tryin' ta ride my bike here!"

Wiggle Puppy exclaimed, "Arf! Arf! Rowl! Arf!" That was his way of saying, "Caution, sir! It is illegal and foolish to ride a bicycle without a helmet!"

The man became very agitated, "Get away from me, ya stupid mutt!"

Wiggle Puppy kept flying in circles around and around the man's head, trying to warn him. The man was so angry, he didn't know he was riding into the Springfield Tire Yard.

The man pedaled right into a cloud of smoke from the burning tires!

"Aw geez!" complained the man. "Look at this! Now I can't see nothin'!"

The man was rubbing his eyes as he rode his bicycle out of the other side of the tire yard and into a gravel company's yard.

"Ruff! Ruff!" warned Wiggle Puppy, which was his way of saying, "Look out, sir! You have a rough road ahead!"

But the man couldn't see. He rode his bicycle over craggy gravel, then up a long chute that led to the roof of a building.

"Roof! Roof!" Wiggle Puppy exclaimed, which was his way of saying, "Have a care, sir! You are now on the roof of a building!"

The man didn't listen. He continued rubbing his eyes and pedaling until he came to the edge of the roof and rode over.

"Yaaaaaah!" yelled the man.

SMASH! The man and his bicycle hit the ground hard.

"Oh geez, that hurt," the man croaked. "Right between the...ah, I'll never be a daddy now." Miraculously, the man didn't fall off his bicycle. He kept pedaling slowly, even though the wheels were warped and the frame bent.

"Gotta ride off the pain...gotta ride off the pain...gotta ride off the pain..!" the man repeated.

Just then, Wiggle Puppy hollered, "Woof! Woof!" which was his way of saying, "Warning, sir! A wolf has escaped from the zoo!"

"Grrrr!" growled the wolf, before tearing a chunk out of the man's leg and running off with it.

"Ah gawd!" the man yelled, and began pedaling faster and faster.

"Bark! Bark!" Wiggle Puppy exclaimed, which was his way of telling the man, "Look out, sir! You are about to hit a tree!"

WHAM! The man fell to the ground, his body bent every which-way. His eyes were red and puffy. He held one mangled hand over his special place. His leg was bleeding profusely.

"Urggggh..." the man said.

Quick as a wink, Wiggle Puppy flew to where an ambulance was parked.

"Vrrrrooom! Arf! Arf! Ruff!" Wiggle Puppy told the paramedics.

"A man down outside the old gravel company?" Paramedic Ruth exclaimed.

"Thanks, Wiggle Puppy," said Paramedic DiMaggio. "We're on it!"

Wiggle Puppy stayed close, as the paramedics gathered up the man and put him in the ambulance.

"Please, just get me the hell away from that weird little dog!" the man screamed, and the paramedics drove away, sirens blaring.

Wiggle Puppy
watched them go,
a proud smile on his face.
Another heroic job by Wiggle Puppy!

"Arf! Arf! Vrooom!"
That was Wiggle Puppy's way of saying,
"Don't get hurt or dead—wear a helmet on your head!"

The End!

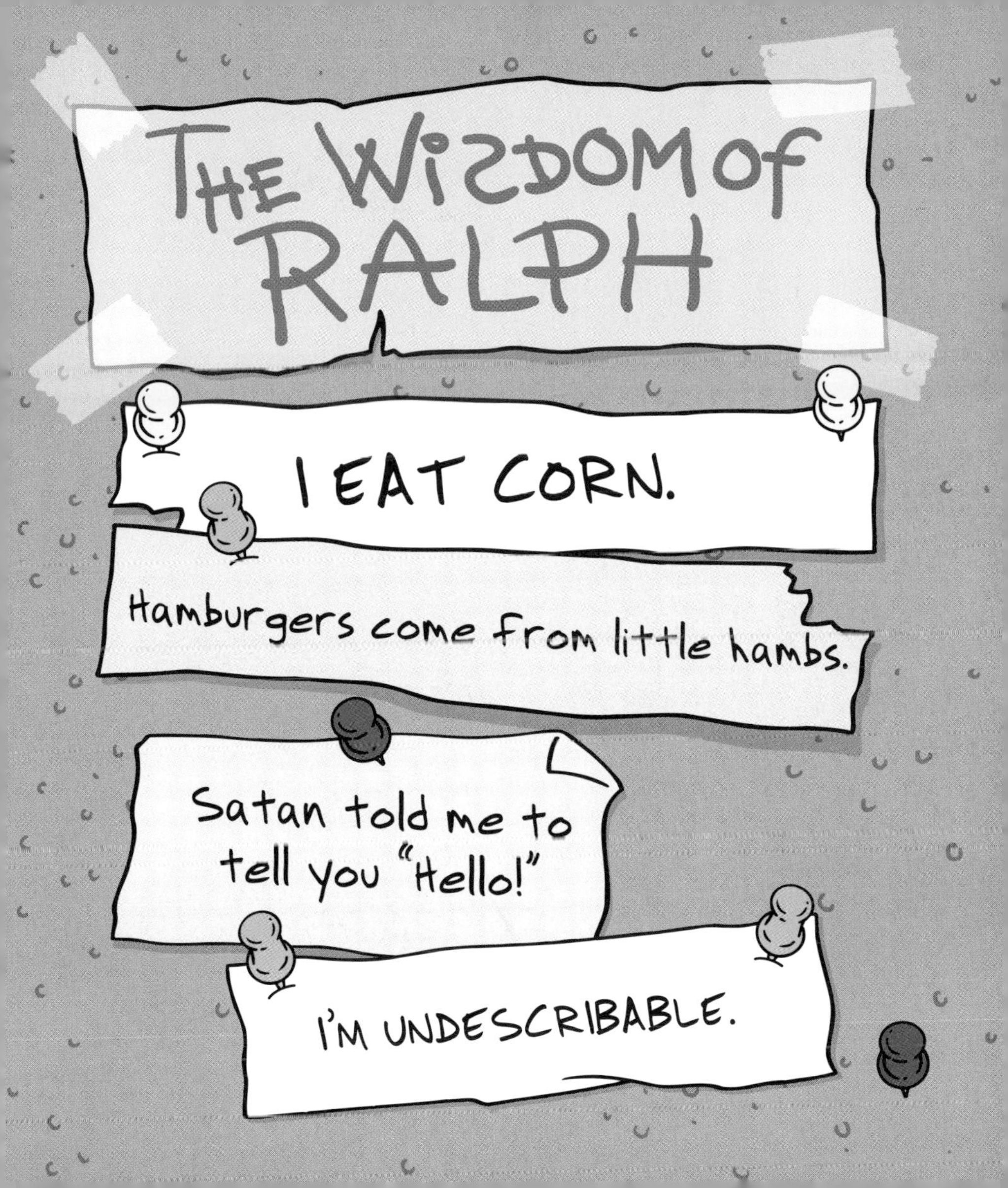
THE WISDOM OF RALPH
I EAT CORN.
Hamburgers come from little hambs.
Satan told me to tell you "Hello!"
I'M UNDESCRIBABLE.

Looking for answers to life's perplexing conundrums? Why not...

Dear Ralph,
How do I know if my wife is cheating on me?
Signed, Wondering

Dear Wondering,
Cheating is wrong! Principal Skinner says your wife should keep her eyes on her own test.

******

Dear Ralph,
I started a long distance romance and fell in love with a man. But the distance between us was too much to bear, so I broke it off to date someone nearer to me. After a few years, that relationship began to develop. But now the first man has moved back into my life! I love them both dearly. How do I pick?
Signed, Torn

Dear Torn,
Fingers are good for picking, especially the pointing finger. A thumb won't fit up your nose.

******

Dear Ralph,
I love my girlfriend, but we've been together for six months, and she won't sleep with me. What should I do?
Signed, Anxious

Dear Anxious,
I used to sleep with Mommy and Daddy. Then I wetted the bed. Now they won't sleep with me, and I sleep in rubber jammies!

*****

Dear Ralph,
My boss keeps making inappropriate comments to me at work. I like working for him, but I think he has a thing for me. Should I sue him or sit on his lap like he asks?
Signed, Harassed

Dear Harassed,
I sat on a man's lap with a red suit and a white beard at the mall! He smelled like Daddy's drunk tank.

*****

ASK RALPH

Dear Ralph,
A few years ago, my father and I got into a terrible fight. We haven't spoken in ten years, but now he's on his deathbed. I want to mend the bridge between us before he dies. Do you have any advice?
Signed, Apologizing

Dear Apologizing,
Once my daddy found a box of cream donuts in the trunk of his squad car. They had been there a whole year. Daddy ate the whole box and spent all day in bed. Then his guts got into a fight and his stomach cried out all the donuts.

******

Dear Ralph,
Last week at my poker game I won the last kitty. When I counted it, it came up short. I can't believe my friends would steal from me, but I'm very sure of the count. Should I say anything to them?
Signed, Cheated

Dear Cheated,
My kitty is big, too. I counted that it ate ten bugs once. I ate three!

Club Calendar
By Club Correspondent Fred Newman

Sunday:
The Parents with Hyper-Active Teenagers (PHT) Support Group will meet at 5:30 p.m. at the rear of the Springfield Police Station to identify their teens in police lineups. A covered-dish supper will be served.

The Springfield Astronomy Club will meet with telescopes ready. 9 p.m. across the street from the Fiesta Terrace Apartments. Discussion group to follow.

Monday:
The Bulbous Nose Club will have group therapy and fellowship in Lamar Tutwill's Winnebago, parked at the intersection of Main and Colonial. Members are encouraged to bring quarters for the parking meter.

Brotherhood of People Who Wear Adjustable Mesh Caps With Farm Equipment Logos will meet in the back room of Herman's Military Antiques to watch Tractor Pull on ESPN. Bring stuff to throw at TV. No loaded firearms over .30 caliber, please.

Wednesday:
All-day sign-ups for the Bowlers with Skin Rash League at Barney's Bowlarama. Bowlers with chaffing and prickly heat needed. Please bring bowling gloves – we don't want to spread anything.

1. **Mr. Sun-Dried Tomato Man!** It's like when my grandpa growed older. Before, he was plump and happy. Now he's shrively and smells funny.
2. **The Holey Bad Man!** When it gets windy, he whistles. Sometimes Daddy gets surprised, and forgets he's there, and shoots more holes in him.
3. **Robby the Rocket Ship!** He takes me to the Moon and smells like thrown-up M&Ms inside.
4. **Lawn Darts!** They used to be pointy on their ends, but now they're not. Mommy and Daddy took me to the hospital, and the doctor found the points in my head.
5. **Horny Toad!** Only, Daddy says to call him "Get It On" Toad, because "horny" is a bad word. He used to crawl around a lot, but now he's always sleeping. I painted him purple!
6. **Toy Chunk!** After a while, my toys got stuck together somehow. Mommy says it's the fault of ice cream and jelly.
7. **The Leprechaun!** He tells me to burn things. Last week, he promised me a pot of gold if I would shoot Daddy's flare gun in the Teachers' Lounge.
8. **My First Bullhorn!** It turns your indoor voice into a big voice like the "Clean-up on aisle five" Man.
9. **Big Drum-Drum!** When I play it, small meteors from our neighbors' yard fall out of the sky!
10. **The Mud Puppy!** Daddy says every time I pet him and hold him Bactine's stock goes up 5%.
11. **Springy the Horsey!** He likes to fall over when I climb on. Daddy says if he gets any less springy, he's gonna have to put him down for good.
12. **My Sandbox!** I'm not supposed to use it like a cat's sandbox. Mommy says big boys can hold it until they go inside.
13. **Bart Simpson!** But he only comes over to play "Hide Ralph in the prickly bushes"--or when Daddy gets a new supply of tear gas canisters.

THE WISDOM OF RALPH
Bitey things are niceless.
I saw Honolulu out the window.
My other mommy went to the squirrel farm.
Pop music is hard work.

ANATOMY OF RALPH

1. **HAIRSTYLE** – The classic bowl cut. Only The Three Stooges' Moe wore it better.
2. **EYES** – Both lazy.
3. **BRAIN** – Where dreams of being a Viking and little else reside.
4. **NOSE** – A.k.a. The Booger Vault.
5. **FINGERS** – Keys to The Booger Vault.
6. **EARS** – Manufacturer and container of wax, for those lean and hungry times when paste is not available.
7. **TONGUE** – Discerner of Ralph's least favorite tastes (burning and Grandma) and his favorite crayon flavor (red).
8. **HEART** – Broken when Lisa didn't "choo-choo-choose" him.
9. **FIGURE** – Like father, like son.
10. **TUMMY** – Usual contents: paste, crayons, cap gun caps, worms (gummy and regular), more paste, instrument knobs and dials, a thumbtack, plastic french fries from Krusty Burger playset.
11. **BELT** – Pulled extra-tight to deter wedgies.
12. **POCKETS** – Home of lint buddies Myrtle, Jo Jo, and Ralph Junior.
13. **PANTS** – Stain-proof. Flame retardant. Stylish.
14. **RUBBER UNDERPANTS** – To be worn until he learns.
15. **SHOES** – Extra-wide non-skid loafers for convenience, safety, and balance.

RALPH'S GUIDE TO CONSTELLATIONS

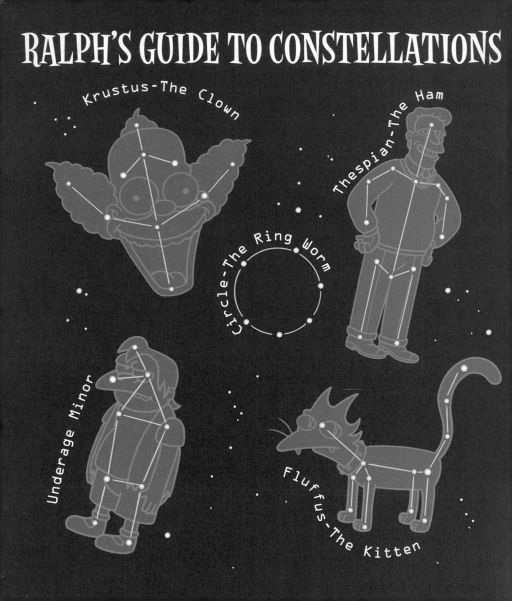

Krustus-The Clown

Thespian-The Ham

Circle-The Ring Worm

Underage Minor

Fluffus-The Kitten

RALPH'S DREAM HOUSE

1. Piranha pond: one fish kissed two of my toes off.
2. Garden: a place to grow catnip for Mittens and bones for Wiggle Puppy.
3. Veranda: a place to sip nonalcoholic mint tulips.
4. Cat door: for Mittens to come and go. Mostly she goes.
5. Wiggle Puppy doghouse.
6. Tower: when I catch one, I'll put a princess up there!
7. Stairway to Nowhere.
8. Attic of Terror: I only go in there with my rubber pants on.
9. Bedroom: where I have my Viking dreams!
10. Leprechaun guest room: asbestos-lined for when he makes me burn things.
11. Bathroom: with ejector potty seat for when I forget to get off.
12. Escalator ride with or without safety pillows: either way, I go to sleep when I land!
13. Crayon Art Studio: crayons are a good source of vitamin wax!
14. Emergency room: I use it every day!
15. Panic room: a place to go after visiting the Attic of Terror.
16. Home theater: I saw a movie where some naked people wouldn't let each other go to sleep.
17. Kitchen with gas stove: Owie! Bart told me blue fire would be cold!
18. Gym with treadmill: I can run and run without going anywhere--unless I stop running. Then I fly like Superman!
19. Library: books are scratch and sniff or washable.
20. Juice cellar: with many vintages of juice boxes.
21. Hot tub: for relaxation and boiling potatoes.
22. Recording studio: for recording solo follow-up to Party Posse CD.

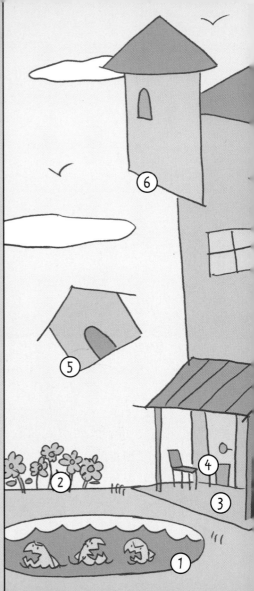

We live in a country in which any child could grow up to be President. Imagine if one of these young people didn't grow up to be President but rather, was elected TODAY? And imagine if that wee one was RALPH WIGGUM? What changes would come to our beloved land? Let us posit some answers to the unthinkable question...

...WHAT IF RALPH WIGGUM WAS ELECTED PRESIDENT?

- Jellybeans would be recognized as a valid form of currency (except the black ones).
- Barney Gumble would be the Secretary of Burpy Noises.
- The Wiggles "Willaby Wallaby Woo" would now be the United States national anthem.
- The colored sugar juice in wax candy bottles would flow freely from water fountains.
- Banisters would always be greased, making it impossible to get your head stuck in them.
- All waistbands would be elastic.
- Buildings would have to be painted purple because "Purple is fun!"
- No words would be allowed to be over two syllables––and the word syllable would be changed to "blops."
- There would be the immediate implementation of the Wiggum Purchase to make Candyland the 51st state.
- The fifty-one states would be consolidated into three because "Fifty-one is impossible to remember."
- First time felons, instead of facing jail time, would be put in yearlong "time outs."

- The FAA would be put in charge of all paper airplanes.
- Everything would come with sprinkles.
- Archie would finally be forced to choose between Betty and Veronica.
- Disney would finally have to make a sequel to "Pete's Dragon."
- The only acceptable form of fast travel on foot would be skipping.
- All steaks would come pre-cut in bite-sized pieces.
- Bath days would be once a month.
- No more acronyms.
- A fourth "R" would be introduced to contemporary American education: Ring toss.
- The inventor of the brussels sprout would be hunted down, captured, and forced to eat "a lot of them because they taste so bad."
- Sideshow Mel would be named head of the Department of Hairdo Security.
- Snack-time would be made an official meal.
- Escalators would be replaced with rideable rainbows.
- No more wars: potato sack races and bake-offs would be used to solve world conflicts.
- The United States would move toward a parliamentary system of government.
- A Big Wheel lane would be incorporated into all public roadways.
- Whenever requested, adults would have to tell children stories.
- There would be an immediate ban on all mega-soaker, long-range assault water guns.
- Emergency underwear would be available in all businesses and public buildings.
- There would be gum especially made for dogs.
- Shoelaces would be eliminated in favor of Velcro for all shoes.
- There would be a Poison Control Center on every block, specializing in the ingestion of dice, powdered hand soap, and action figures.
- The typical American greeting would be changed from the handshake to hugging oneself and smiling.

RALPHIE WIGGUM Living

HOMEMADE HOLIDAY CRAFTS

Father's Day Tie-Dye Ties:
Take one of your dad's ties and mix together tomato sauce, grape juice, mustard, motor oil, and bleach and see what happens. If nothing blows up, wrap a rubber band around the tie and dip it into the mixture. If it does blow up, try it without the mustard.

Valentine's Day Rock Box:
Buy a heart-shaped box of Valentine's chocolate. Eat the chocolate. Paint small rocks and put them in each of the paper cups. Give to your sweetie to find out how much she likes rocks.

Easter Bonnet:
Take a tissue box and remove the tissues. Paint them and dip them in perfume. Then wad them into flowerish-looking balls and glue them to the tissue box. Tell your mom to wear this to church on Easter or you'll cry.

St. Patrick's Day Shamrocks:
When your mom makes coffee, ask her for three filters. It's better if they're green, leaf-shaped ones. It's also better if she drinks her coffee first, or she might yell. Glue them together, plant them on your lawn, and look out for leprechauns!

Mother's Day Soap Porcupines:
Get a bar of soap and stick pins or toothpicks or needles or something that looks like those things that stick out of porcupines into it. Just don't let your mom wash her face with it! Soap can dry a woman's skin.

Thanksgiving Hand Turkeys Placemats:
For each place at your dining room table, trace your hand with a marker. Draw in details to make your thumb a turkey head and your three fingers its tail. If you can remember, put a piece of paper under your hand or these placemats won't move.

Fourth of July Fireworks:
Save the volatile mustard version of the Father's Day tie-dye mixture and pour it into empty toilet paper rolls. Insert a string or shoelace and light it. Make sure that you always light fireworks with a parent or other adult or a bigger kid who has all his fingers.

Hanukkah/Fourth of July Menorah:
Instead of boring candles, use leftover 4th of July Fireworks. Now each day of Hanukkah is sure to be a Festival of Light and Smoke and Piercing Eardrum Damage.

New Year's Paper Hat:
Glue construction paper into a cone hat. Glue confetti to the hat. Glue the hat on your head. At midnight, run around. After a while, your dad will put the hat in a shredder. Save that confetti to glue onto next year's hat!

Halloween Caramel Apples:
Melt some caramel. You can also buy pre-melted caramel. Stick sticks into a bunch of apples. You can also buy pre-sticked apples. Dip the sticked apple into the caramel. You can also buy pre-made caramel apples. They're much better.

President's Day Lincoln Costume:
Get some hair or fur! Glue it to a strip of paper and glue the paper to your chin. Glue a roll of paper towels to a paper plate to make a stovepipe hat and dip it in ordinary black household paint. Put the costume on and see how many people you can emancipate!

Christmas Pretzel Wreath:
Get a box of pretzels, lime gelatin, maraschino cherries, and common school paste. Paste all the pretzels into a wreath-shaped wreath, coat it in green gelatin, and attach a few cherries. The best part is if you get hungry, you can eat the paste!

Ralph Identifies the Twenty Types of Grown-ups

RALPH'S SUMMER VACATION

MY SUMMER VACATION WAS THREE MONTHS AWAY FROM THE SCHOOL. WHEN MISS HOOVER AND THE OTHER KIDS STOPPED SHOWING UP FOR CLASS, SO DID I. MY DADDY AND I SPENT LOTS OF TIME TOGETHER 'CAUSE MOMMY SAYS I *"STRESS HER OUT."*

FIRST, WE WENT TO THE BEACH ALL DAY. MY SKIN GOT SORE AND RED AND DADDY SWALLOWED LOTS OF WATER. THREE WHOLE CRABS WENT IN HIS MOUTH AND WOULDN'T COME OUT.

THEN WE WENT TO THE HOSPITAL WHERE I SAT IN A CHAIR WITH WHEELS.

THE NEXT WEEK, AFTER DADDY FELT BETTER, HE TOOK ME TO THE PETTING ZOO. I MADE FRIENDS WITH LOTS OF ANIMALS. DADDY SAID HE JUST GOT PAID AND HAD A WALLET FULL OF LETTUCE, SO I BORROWED IT AND FED THE LETTUCE TO A HUNGRY GOAT. DADDY GOT MAD AND WE WENT ALL THE WAY HOME.

WHEN DADDY GOT UNMAD, WE DROVE TO THE WOODS TO GO CAMPING. THERE WAS NO TV FOR MILES SO WE MADE A FIRE. WHEN I GOT CLOSE TO IT, IT MADE MY FACE SMELL LIKE BACON! LATER, WE MET A BEAR WHO WAS ANGRY AT DADDY FOR BEING A HUMAN. DADDY GOT IN THE CAR JUST IN THE NICK OF TIME AND WE DROVE AWAY. I STILL DON'T KNOW WHO *NICK* IS.

FOR THE REST OF THE SUMMER, WE RELAXED AT HOME WHERE DADDY WOULDN'T GET SCARED OR MAD OR HURT. IT WAS THE BEST SUMMER I HAD ALL YEAR.

THE END!

RALPH'S BEDROOM

1. Ant Farm. (Ralph let the ants escape, so his dad replaced them with black jellybeans.)
2. My First Police Radio®.
3. Homework easel.
4. Man in the Moon night light. (Sometimes he and Ralph tell each other secrets.)
5. Pictures taken at his daddy's work.
6. Light-blocking curtains. (Very handy--if they're closed during the day, Ralph will go to sleep!)
7. Officer Bear. (He guards Ralph's other stuffed animals.)
8. Hamper for used "little boy underpants."
9. Hamper for when Ralph has a "big boy night."
10. Shrine to Lisa Simpson.
11. Homemade fun ball area. (Ralph gets lost and cries hysterically every time he goes in there.)
12. Mr. Turtle Chair. (Which explains why Ralph sits on every turtle he sees, even the tiny ones.)
13. Toy Chest. (All the toys inside are sticky and the ants from the farm live in there.)
14. Where "Uh-ohs" happened.
15. The mailman. (Sometimes Ralph practices police tactics his dad taught him on strangers who come to the door.)
16. Jack Webb bedspread. (A hand-me-down from Chief Wiggum.)
17. Ralph's nighttime helmet. (So he doesn't hurt himself when he falls out of bed.)
18. Wiggle Puppy drawing collection, including painting by LeRoy Neiman, who passed through Springfield once and was pulled over for a broken taillight.

A MEGA-COLLECTION OF THE BIGGEST AND BEST FROM RALPH'S GALAXY OF MISHEARD HIT SONGS

YOU'LL HEAR CHART-BUSTING FAVORITES LIKE:

KBBL

Elvis Costello's EVERY DAY I RIDE THE BUS

Jose Feliciano's POLICE NABBED MY DAD

The Ramones' I WANNA PIECE O' DAVID

Prince's I WOULD DIAPER YOU

The Beatles' LUCY IN DISGUISE WITH LINUS

Squeeze's PULLING MUSTARD FROM MICHELLE

ABBA's JACKIE CHAN'S ON ME

Elton John's (HOLD ME CLOSER,) TONY DANZA

The Four Tops' AIN'T NO WOMAN LIKE A ONE-EYED GOAT

Queen's ANOTHER ONE BUYS THE DUCKS

5th Dimension's (THIS IS THE DROWNING OF THE) ANCIENT AQUARIUMS

The Rolling Stones' (I'LL NEVER BE YOUR) BIG SUBURBAN

Michael Jackson's BILLIE JEAN (JUST SHOT MY LLAMA)

Bob Dylan's (THE ANTS ARE MY FRIENDS AND) BLOWIN' IN THE WIND

Eddie Money's TWO CHICKENS TO PARALYZE

The Go-Gos' I LICKED A SEAL

Aerosmith's DO THE FUNKY LADY

AND MANY MORE!

ART D'RALPH:
The Masterpieces of Young Master Wiggum

Daddy's Keys Glued to a Piece of Wood

Medium: Keys on scrap lumber, Eterno-bond brand adhesive (includes keys to the Wiggum house, several police cruisers, cells in the Springfield Jail, and safe deposit box #357 at the Springfield National Bank). Gift of Ralph Wiggum.

Blueberry Doggie-Woggie

Medium: Generic purple crayon on living room wall. Permanent installation of the Wiggum Family Collection.

Broken Fun Thing

Medium: GBox-II video game
system with Krusty's
Non-Dairy Non-Ice Cream Whey
Product Sandwich.
Collection of the
Martin Prince rumpus room,
pending donation to the Springfield
Sanitation Department.

Happy Face Happy Days

Medium: "Happy Days"
Season One DVDs,
permanently scratched
with a paring knife.
Gift of the
Springfield Sanitation
Department.

Glass Door Owie

Medium: Perspiration, skin oils
on glass.
Permanent installation of the
Wiggum patio.

My School at Sunset

Medium: Oils on canvas (with one ketchup packet). Painted shortly after accidentally taking another student's Ritalin. Permanent installation of the C. Montgomery Burns collection.

Brockman in Space!

Medium: Brand new Sanshiba widescreen HDTV (retail price: $7,500.00), two months old, with Forever Mark'd brand permanent marker. Drawn during a segment of "Smartline with Kent Brockman." Currently on display at Hard Decisions Appliance Repair— "The Eighty-Bucks-Just-to-Look-at-It People!"

Bent Microwaved Wookie

Medium: Original "Star Wars" Chewbacca action figure, altered by heat and blunt impact. On loan from the Milhouse Collection.

I Was Looking at a Bird for a Long Time

Medium: Sidewalk concrete,
Tootsie-Town brand shoes.
Permanent installation
of the Evergreen Terrace
sidewalk collection.

Sunday, After Sundae

Medium: The artist, Ralph Wiggum;
a Gooey Chewy Peanut Buttery Fudgey Wudge
Ice Cream Supreme Sundae from Cody Sugarcone's
Ice Cream Corral; good church clothes
from Chumley the Fox Suits for Boys.
On loan to Dr. Stainsbegone Dry Cleaners.

Daddy Jailbird

Medium: PickyChrome 500 film, taken with the
Springfield Police Department
Homicide Division camera, shortly
after the creation of
"Daddy's Keys Glued to a Piece of Wood."
Currently on display in the Springfield Police
Department break room.

Ralph's
PLEDGE OF ALLEGIANCE

★ ★ ★

I fudge a legions,

To the flack,

Of the enlightened

skates of a merry cup.

And two derrick public,

Four witches dance,

One Asian,

Underground,

In the visible,

With liver tea and

just us for owl.

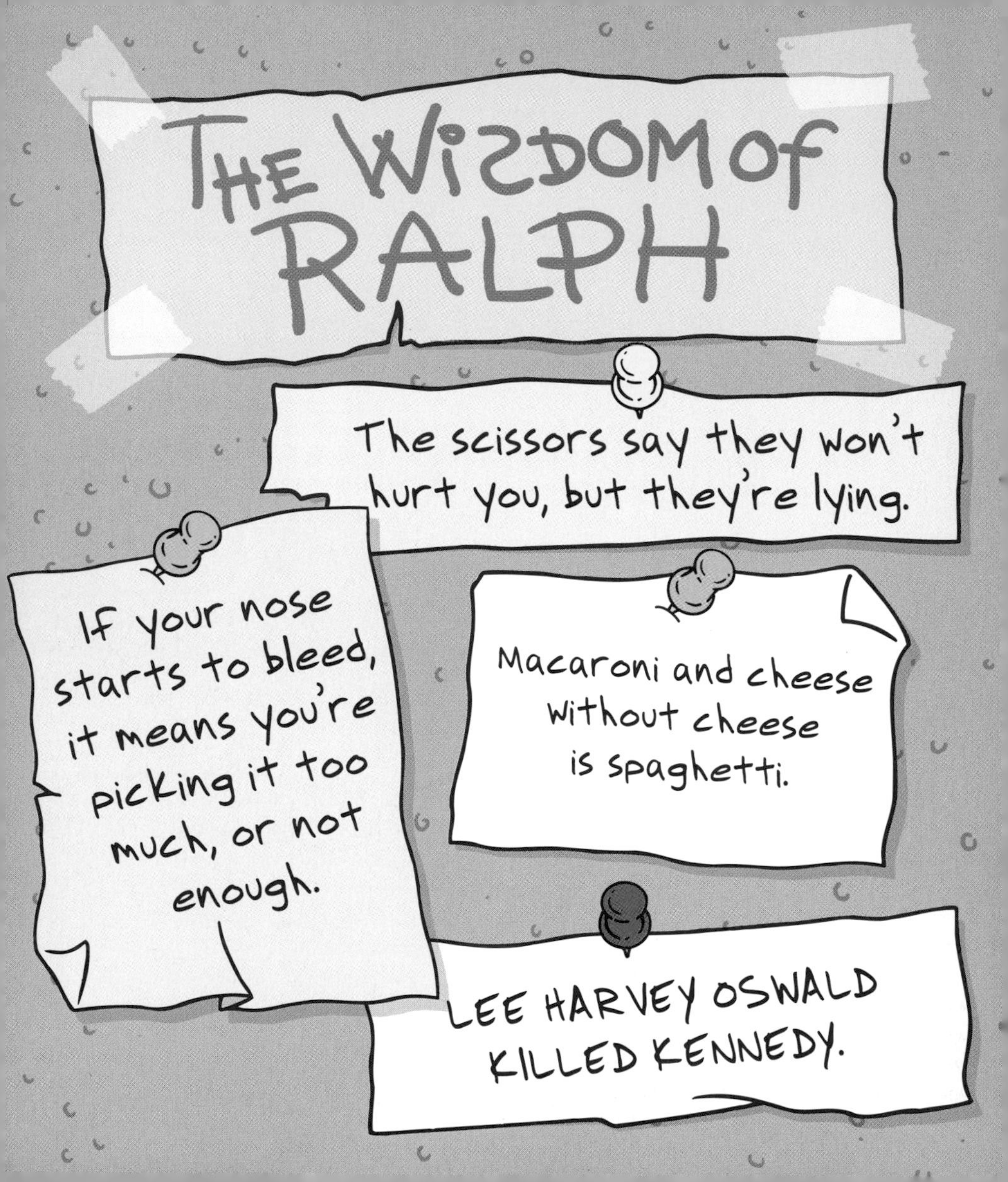
THE WISDOM OF RALPH
The scissors say they won't hurt you, but they're lying.
If your nose starts to bleed, it means you're picking it too much, or not enough.
Macaroni and cheese without cheese is spaghetti.
LEE HARVEY OSWALD KILLED KENNEDY.

I, RALPH WIGGUM, DO SOLEMNLY SWEAR...

I will wrestle only for the purpose of athletic competition and not just to hug people.

I will only eat food.

I will keep my specialness to myself and not tell people I'm special every twenty minutes.

I will not pretend I'm a poo-poo kitty when I play in my sandbox.

I will make friends with my shadow, even if it is trying to kill me.

I will not save my gum for tomorrow by putting it on my head.

I will remember that a matchbook is not the kind of book you do a book report on.

I will always find the best place to throw up, and never in Apu's "Leave a Penny" dish.

I will not look at the sun.

I will always wear my clothes at school.

I will not mistake Groundskeeper Willie's bucket for a potty.

I will not cry when Miss Hoover calls on me.

I will not share my pills with the cat.

I will not taste my shoes.

I will not taste the cat.

I will not taste my classmates.

I will not cut my own hair.

I will not cut my own hair, even to get the gum out.

I will not keep eating after my tummy has an owie.

I will not sleep with my eyes open in class.

I will stop calling Miss Hoover "Mommy."

I will only finger paint on paper, and only with paint.

I will not wear Daddy's underpants as a cape.

I will not stick crayons in my nose or any other hole on my body.

I will not lick other children's plates.

I will not eat a big breakfast before long field trip bus rides.

I will not put chocolate chips in my pockets.

I will not ask to have my mouth washed out with soap every time I solemnly swear, only when I say words like "caca." Oops!

25 cool Things to Be When You Grow up!

1.) Milkman (Like Daddy)
2.) R2-D2 or C-3PO
3.) Lawn Gnome
4.) Fruit of the Loom Banana
5.) Principal
6.) Caterpillar
7.) Air Plane driver
8.) Pop Sensation (again)
9.) Chocolate Candy Conveyor Belt Worker
10.) SnagglePuss
11.) Mario Bros.

12.) Snowman

13.) Hamburger Helper

14.) Owie Doctor

15.) Bowling Pin

16.) Sideshow Ralph

17.) Secretary of Gnomeland Security

18.) Pudding Tester

19.) Shock Jock

20.) traffic Cone

21.) Muffin Man

22.) Cabin Boy

23.) Ghost Buster

24.) Assistant Easter Bunny

25.) Mr. Lisa Simpson

RALPHIE'S SCRAPBOOK

Compiled by Sarah and Clancy Wiggum

Ralphie loves his baths. He gets dirty so often, it's kinda easier to just keep him in the bath from the time he gets home until he goes to bed.

After Ralphie's bad experience at the barber, we started giving him haircuts while he sleeps.

For every birthday after this one, we decided to just give him the wrapping paper.

The first time Ralphie did this, it was cute, but after seven years of it, I'm starting to get a little weirded out. I can't help but flinch when he tries to kiss me goodnight.

I really wish "Kojak" had warmed up to the baby like the dog in "Lady and the Tramp." You know, Lady, not the Tramp. Tramp was cool, though. Man, that dog played by his own rules. Great flick!

These are Ralphie's photos. Technically, this kind of stuff would be considered "invasion of privacy," but with me being the police chief and all, no one says squat. Ralph's free to stalk the girl of his dreams.

Ah, father-son quality time. The walnuts didn't stand a chance.

I only colored outside the lines once! Ralph wasn't hungry when the meal came on account of eating so many crayons.

Ralph's first owie. The first of many to follow.

The people of North Haverbrook were kind enough to return him when he finally landed.

A memento of the first and last time Ralphie was allowed to have pure cane sugar. Let's just say, you can still see his hand prints on the ceiling of Greasy Joe's Bottomless Bar-B-Q Pit.

The Happy Little Elves Enjoy Each Other's Company

The Happy Little Elves' Happy Little Picnic

The Happy Little Elves 2: The Legend of Doofy's Gold

Go, Dog. Go! The Movie

The only one of these movies that didn't give Ralphie nightmares was "Go, Dog. Go!" but I felt that the plot was uneven and that the acting was stilted.

Man...hungry cross-dressing wolves freak me out!

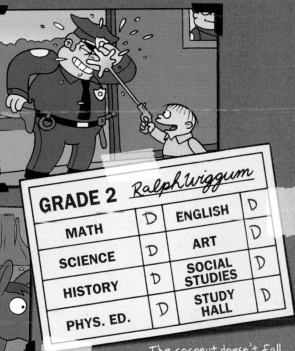

Don't worry. I was out of ammo.

Our first and last trip to the Grand Canyon. Luckily, the donkey broke Ralph's fall. Brave, brave little guy.

GRADE 2	*Ralph Wiggum*			
MATH	D	ENGLISH	D
SCIENCE	D	ART	D
HISTORY	D	SOCIAL STUDIES	D
PHYS. ED.	D	STUDY HALL	D

The coconut doesn't fall far from the tree.

Ralph's 2nd Grade Progress Report

SPRINGFIELD ELEMENTARY SCHOOL PROGRESS REPORT

TEACHER ___Miss. Hoover___

STUDENT: ___Ralph Wiggum___

Reading - Comprehension and Fluency
Needs improvement. He often "forgets how books work," not
understanding the basic mechanics of opening them and turning the
pages.

Chooses appropriate reading materials for
independent reading.
Needs improvement. His "books" of choice continue to be placemats,
empty peanut butter jars with pictures of cartoon characters, and
notes pinned to his clothing.

Uses grammar appropriately.
Needs improvement. Ralph puts "ing" on verbs and nouns,
indiscriminately. Trying to say multisyllable words has often caused
him to pass out and/or get nosebleeds.

Writes legibly.
Satisfactory. Though his letter forms are quite easily discerned,
they are rarely arranged in the proper order to make actual words.

Uses correct punctuation and capitalization.
Needs improvement. Though Ralph has a "big letters go first"
sticker on his desk, he rarely remembers to capitalize. If he
punctuates a sentence (and that's a BIG "if") he only uses giant
exclamation points.

Listening/Speaking
Needs improvement. Ralph answers math questions with information
about his pets and/or pants. He refuses to make anything but
buzzing noises during spelling bees. He often calls me "Mom," "school
Mom," or "glasses lady."

Uses maps effectively.
Needs improvement. Ralph uses maps to blow his nose, as impromptu kilts, and to hide under during thunderstorms.

Mathematics - Understands the value of whole numbers up to 10,000.
Needs improvement. Ralph gets a headache when working with any number over sixteen.

Follows both addition and subtraction facts.
Needs improvement. Ralph attempted to cut off a couple of his fingers (thankfully using safety scissors) while trying to subtract 2 from 5 during a math quiz.

Science - Conducts simple investigations and experiments to test a hypothesis and record results.
Satisfactory. Ralph has conquered using the magnifying glass and has successfully grown a potato. I recommend that Ralph be encouraged in the potato farming arts.

Collects, organizes, and interprets data.
Needs improvement. Ralph only collects the stickers from other children's apples, "shiny gum wrappers, and Bart Simpson's self-published line of "America's Worst Teachers" trading cards.

P.E. - Puts forth effort toward developing skill and improving fitness.
Satisfactory. Though ball-and-rule-based games have eluded Ralph's understanding, we have allowed him to chase butterflies for hours at a time with good results.

Study Skills - Stays focused on task at hand.
This has never happened.

Asks pertinent questions.
Needs improvement. Ralph has, on more than one occasion, raised his hand to ask what Mrs. Wiggum was making for dinner that night or when his favorite television program was coming on.

Notes:
Though the above doesn't quite reflect it, Ralph has come a long way this semester. He no longer eats eraser dust. Alas, Ralph still starts the day by reminding myself and his classmates that everybody poops, he inappropriately asks me and others for hugs and boo-boo kisses, and he has managed to choke on soft ice cream three times. The crayon eating continues.

The Springfield Elementary Puma Press

FREE FOR STUDENTS

SECOND SEMESTER

Me, Ralph

A theater review by Lisa Simpson

It has been said "All the world's a stage"; yesterday afternoon, in the Springfield Elementary cafeteria, the stage was all Ralph Wiggum's world, as he transported the audience to his strange, simple domain, where soap is considered a delicacy and bedtime comes at 4:30 P.M.

"Me, Ralph" is a free-form, mostly improvised, one man show that came out of young master Wiggum's trauma therapy sessions with school psychologist Dr. J. Loren Pryor after the unfortunate incident with Gary the Hamster and the Slinky. In the playbill, Dr. Pryor describes the play as "a journey of self discovery, self expression, and, finally, self actualization." Ralph sums it up more succinctly: "I wear tights!"

And wear tights he does, as well as a sunflower costume, a zoot suit getup, and something that makes him look like a giant fried ravioli. Indeed, wardrobe seemed to be the only planning that went into the show, making it seem somewhat like an Elton John concert without music, cognitive reasoning, or fabulousness. There is no script, no direction, lighting consisted of a Lite Brite duct-taped to the wall, and the only musical accompaniment came from Nelson Muntz (probably to prevent him from heckling), vocalizing his "Haw, haws!" with rhythm and melody, like a bizarre, hyper-affirmative Bobby McFerrin.

During the performance I witnessed Ralph shoving crayons up his nose, engaging in hysterical laughter while looking at a mirror, and repeatedly telling the audience he likes sea horses.

The greatest strength of this show is also its greatest weakness—a journey through the mind of Ralph Wiggum is a hilarious, sweet journey, but it is also a place of maddening stupidity, seemingly impossible ignorance, and frighteningly odd obsessions. Whereas seeing Ralph pretend to be a butterfly is a gentle celebration of his enduring innocence, seeing him violently cry for seven minutes straight after dropping his ice cream cone is simply too much to ask the audience to bear. While I enjoyed his interpretation of Hamlet's speech ("To be a bee or not to be a bee…"), I could do without his "Chew and Show" onstage food review segment. Also, the several times he told me he loved me from onstage made me uncomfortable.

This show does not answer the question "Who is Ralph Wiggum?" Rather it poses countless other queries—the most important being, "Can I actually sit through this?" Attend a performance and answer that question for yourself.

A carrot stick, lukewarm apple juice, and a Hannukah candle smeared with apple butter are served at intermission.

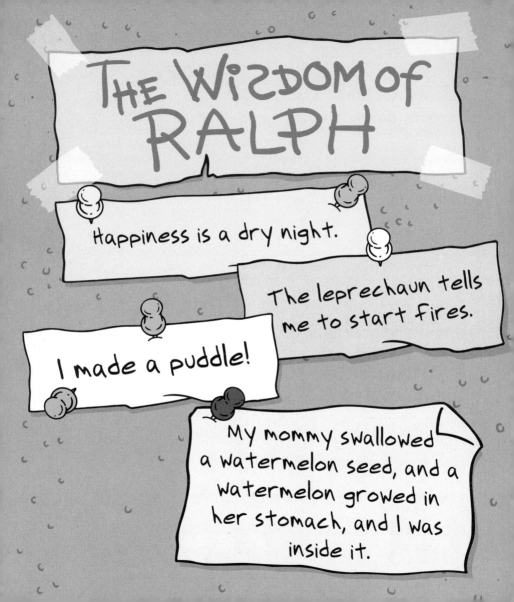

RALPH'S GOTTA-SEE TV LINE-UP

7   7 A.M. **JCTV**
HOUR OF GUILT AND SHAME (Religion) 60 min.

12   8 A.M. **MORE-ON TV**
THE TERRIBLE TOONS (Animated) 60 min. Incredibly bad writing finds its match with poorly drawn characters and backgrounds.

4   9 A.M. **STUPIDSTATION**
MOPMAN AND UNDERPANTS (Animated) 30 min. Mopman finds that nothing goes righty when your whiteys are too tighty.

163   9:30 A.M. **MORE-ON TV**
SUPER SULLEN TEEN AVENGERS (Animated) 60 min. Petulant teenage superheroes fight crime and, like, intense boredom, okay?

18   10:30 A.M. **TOON OUT NETWORK**
PAWS & WHISKERS (Animated) 30 min. Worldwide panic ensues when a bunch of creepy little kittens take over the Tokyo stock exchange.

213   11 A.M. **THE ENGLISH CHANNEL**
WEE WALLY WANKLE'S MAGICAL FUNTASTIC RAINBOW EXPRESS (Edutainment) 30 min. Join Wally on a rollicking, fun-filled tour of the letters K through M.

17   11:30 A.M. **KIDS' SHOPPING CHANNEL**
BUY ME THAT! (Product placement) 30 min.

12 12:00 P.M. **EMPTY VEE**
TOP 10 COUNTDOWN (Filler) 30 min. Countdown of the top ten numbers.

32 12:30 P.M. **BAD B O**
HOLLYWOOD HAS-BEENS STRIP POKER SHOWDOWN (Pathetic) 90 min. Obscure celebrities and former sitcom stars vie for your attention.

6 2:00 P.M. **TOTAL BSTV**
POVERTY FACTOR (Reality) 30 min. Poor folks go head to head in an extreme competition for food and shelter.

4 2:30 P.M. **STUPIDSTATION**
UNDERWATER NUN (Religious Comedy) 30 min. Sister Aquanetta prays for surf.

6 3 P.M. **TOTAL BSTV**
THIS FILTHY OLD RAT HOLE (Home Improvement) 30 min. Host Bob Beeler tours America's most repugnant homes.

573 3:30 P.M. **BLAH CHANNEL**
THE BUNDY BUNCH (Dramedy) 30 min. Ted gets into hot water with the sheriff.

104 4 P.M. **RERUNLAND**
KISS & HUGGS (Crime Drama) 60 min. Detectives Kiss and Huggs become ensnared in a bad plotline when they go undercover as a pair of crooked cops to uncover a pair of crooked undercover cops.

9 5 P.M. **BOX**
NEWS (Repeat) 30 min.

433 5:30 P.M. **C-SPIN**
WHO CUT THE CHEESE? (Discussion) 30 min.

9 6 P.M. **BOX**
AMERICA'S ZANIEST STORE SURVEILLANCE VIDEOS (Utter Tedium) 60 min.

104 7 P.M. **RERUNLAND**
MUDRER, SHE TYPED (Mystery) 60 min. Jessica whites-out a typo. (First of two parts.)

109 8 P.M. **CHIXFLIX**
MOVIE "MY SISTER MARRIED A NUTJOB" (Sentimental Claptrap) 2 hrs. Based on a shocking true story overheard at the nail salon.

323 10 P.M. **HYDROGEN**
LAWN ORDER (Crime Drama) 30 min. Police hunt for a serial weed killer.

2 10:30 P.M. **ZZZ TV**
THIRTY MINUTES TO KILL (Dead Air) 30 min.

It has been said that those who don't know history are doomed to repeat it. But what of those who sort of know history? Will their misinterpretations of the facts lead to an approximation of historical recurrences? Or will their thin grasp of past events somehow give them enough information to spur their imaginations and thus bring us into a divine age free of strife and human hardship? As Kent Brockman has said over and over again, "Only time will tell." Until then, comfort yourself with...

GREAT MOMENTS IN HISTORY
ACCORDING TO RALPH!

RALPH'S B

1. A BENT WOOKIE.
2. THE DEEP END OF THE SANDBOX.
3. PLASTIC CANDY THAT TASTES LIKE PLASTIC AND NOT LIKE CANDY.
4. SALMON GUTTERERS.
5. BEING UNSPECIAL.
6. MY TOOTHBRUSH.
7. SUPER NINTENDO CHALMERS.
8. BLUE BARF.
9. FUNNY-TASTING KNOBS.
10. A WET BED.
11. SCISSORS THAT BITE.
12. MOMMY'S TUNA FISH CASTEROLL.
13. YUCKY DOO-DOO.
14. NUMBER FIFTYTEEN.
15. FISHSTICKS THAT TASTE LIKE FISH AND NOT LIKE STICKS.
16. CREEPY TREES.
17. BEING FOLLOWED BY A MOONSHADOW.
18. SITTING IN A TINKLE PUDDLE.
19. FORGETTING TO BREATHE.
20. THINGS THAT SQUISH WHEN YOU PET THEM.
21. GETTING CARSICK WHEN I WALK.
22. COOTIES.
23. THINGS THAT GO IN YOUR NOSE AND THEN DON'T COME OUT.
24. GRUMBLY TUMMIES.

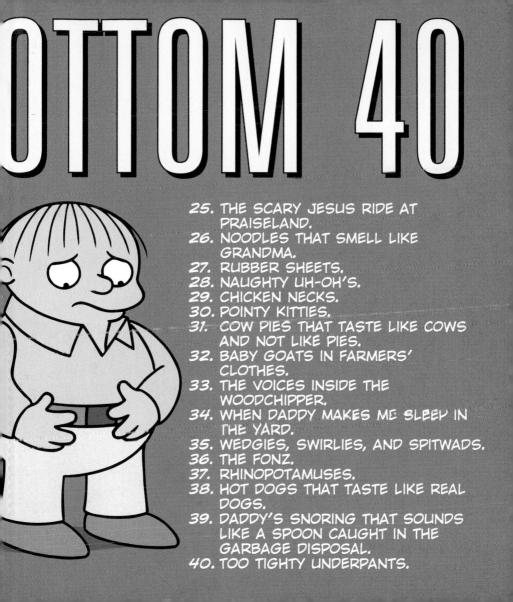

OTTOM 40

25. THE SCARY JESUS RIDE AT PRAISELAND.
26. NOODLES THAT SMELL LIKE GRANDMA.
27. RUBBER SHEETS.
28. NAUGHTY UH-OH'S.
29. CHICKEN NECKS.
30. POINTY KITTIES.
31. COW PIES THAT TASTE LIKE COWS AND NOT LIKE PIES.
32. BABY GOATS IN FARMERS' CLOTHES.
33. THE VOICES INSIDE THE WOODCHIPPER.
34. WHEN DADDY MAKES ME SLEEP IN THE YARD.
35. WEDGIES, SWIRLIES, AND SPITWADS.
36. THE FONZ.
37. RHINOPOTAMUSES.
38. HOT DOGS THAT TASTE LIKE REAL DOGS.
39. DADDY'S SNORING THAT SOUNDS LIKE A SPOON CAUGHT IN THE GARBAGE DISPOSAL.
40. TOO TIGHTY UNDERPANTS.